ENGLISH TODAY!

D H Howe

Oxford University Press

Oxford University Press
Great Clarendon Street, Oxford OX2 6DP

Oxford New York
Athens Auckland Bangkok Bogota Bombay
Buenos Aires Calcutta Cape Town Dar es Salaam
Delhi Florence Hong Kong Istanbul Karachi
Kuala Lumpur Madras Madrid Melbourne
Mexico City Nairobi Paris Singapore
Taipei Tokyo Toronto

and associated companies in
Berlin Ibadan

OXFORD and OXFORD ENGLISH are trade marks of
Oxford University Press

ISBN International Edition 0 19 433186 5
       Egyptian Edition   0 19 436021 0
       Special I.S.E. Edition 0 19 436106 3

© Oxford University Press 1986

First published 1986
Eleventh impression 1997
First published in the Egyptian edition 1993
Fifth impression 1996
First published in the Special I.S.E. edition 1995

Cover photograph by Ian Frazer

Illustrations by: Judith Allibone, John Dyke, Charlotte Firmin,
Elaine Pinnock, Gerald Rose, Graham Round, Barry Rowe,
Sara Silcock, Fran Thatcher, Jenny Thorne,
Anne Winterbottom

The publishers would like to thank the staff and pupils of
Donnington Middle School, Oxford for their help.

Typeset by Oxford Publishing Services

Printed in Hong Kong

The items in the two lists below are included in this book. The numbers refer to the pages on which the items occur. The word 'throughout' means that the item occurs too often to be listed.

Communicative functions

Language items

Measurements

I'm Ben.
I'm 40 kilos.
I'm 120 centimetres.

Ben

Kate

Annie

A
1 How tall is Ben?
2 How heavy is Ben?
3 How tall is Kate?
4 How heavy is Kate?
5 How tall is Annie?
6 How heavy is Annie?

B
1 Kate is taller than _Ben_.
2 Kate is _heavier_ than Ben.
3 Annie is _taller than_ Kate.
4 Annie is _heavier than_ Kate.
5 Ben is _smaller_ than Kate.
6 Kate is _smaller_ than Annie.

weaker
stronger
smaller

spelling! also
thinner taller younger
fatter shorter
bigger older

Revision

Where are they?

Can you see these things in the picture? Where are they?

a fish	a clock	an ice-cream	a spoon	a shoe	a boat
a car	an egg	a radio	a crab	a train	an umbrella

at the top of

at the side of   in the middle of   at the end of

at the bottom of   in front of

There is a fish at the top of the tree.

What is wrong with the picture?

Miss Lake put a picture on the board.
'Draw this,' she said to Mary.
Mary drew her picture.

Miss Lake's picture

Mary's picture

What is wrong with Mary's picture?
There are thirteen things wrong.
Here are two:

The girl's legs are too short.

Can you see the other things?

The dog is too thin.

os ndhorse picture belt
lowers   map   book
pen   socks   map circled
cat   hair

3

Revision

What did they say?

What did Sam say?   What did Susan say?
Read the right number with the right letter.

Sam

1 How old is your father?
2 I'm hungry.
3 Is this yours?
4 How many apples did you eat?
5 How much money have you got?
6 I'm looking for my pen.
7 Let's have a swim.
8 You haven't got much jam, have you?
9 How heavy are you?
10 You haven't got many oranges, have you?

Susan

a. All of them!
b. Forty-five.
c. No, only a little.
d. No, it's too cold.
e. Yes, I am, too. Let's have something to eat.
f. No, it's not mine.
g. Twenty-six kilos.
h. No, only a few.
i. It's on the desk, between the two books.
j. Not much. Have you got any?

A puzzle

A duck behind two ducks.
A duck in front of two ducks.
A duck between two ducks.
How many ducks?

(The answer is on page 7.)

Revision

4

Sam goes shopping.

Sam   May I have an orange, please?
Shopkeeper   Which one?
Sam   The big one.
Shopkeeper   Certainly.
Sam   Thank you.

Sam   Can I have a cake, please?
Shopkeeper   Which one?
Sam   The small one.
Shopkeeper   Here it is.
Sam   Thank you.

Sam   May I have a tin of coffee, please?
Shopkeeper   Certainly, which one?
Sam   The blue one.
Shopkeeper   Certainly.
Sam   Thank you.

Sam   I want a box of chocolates too.
Shopkeeper   Yes, which one?
Sam   The cheap one.
Shopkeeper   Yes, here it is.
Sam   Thank you.

Question: How much money did Sam give the shopkeeper?

5

Whose is it?

A

B

Revision

C

1 You're playing with our ball.

2 No, we're not.
This is ours.
Yours is there.
Look, can't you see it?

3 They're right.
That's theirs and this is ours.

What colour was the boys' ball?

Black/white

Black/yellow

What colour was the girls' ball?

Answer to the puzzle on page 4

This duck is in front of two ducks.

This duck is between two ducks.

This duck is behind two ducks.

The answer is three ducks.

Revision

The bus timetable

Mr. Green asked a lot of questions about the buses but Sam answered them. His answers are in the wrong order. Can you read Mr. Green's questions and Sam's answers? The bus timetable is on page 9.

When does the first bus leave the ferry?

Does the first bus stop at the park?

What time does the second bus get to the market?

Does the second bus stop at the hospital?

When does the third bus leave the hotel?

Does the third bus stop at the hospital?

What time does the fourth bus leave the hotel?

Yes, it does. It gets there at six twenty-five.

Yes, it does. It gets there at eight o'clock.

It doesn't stop at the hotel.

It leaves the hotel at twenty-five to eight.

At half past seven.

No, it doesn't.

Six o'clock.

Revision

Timetable

Ferry	6.00	6.30	7.00	7.30
Old Street	6.10	6.40	7.10	7.40
Park	6.25	6.55	7.25	7.55
New Street	6.30	7.00	7.30	8.00
Hotel	6.35	7.05	7.35	—
Playground	6.40	7.10	7.40	8.05
Hospital	7.00	—	8.00	8.25
Market	7.10	7.30	8.10	8.35

The seasons in Britain

Finish the sentences. Use these words:

always	usually	cool	sometimes	never	windy

cold	often	warm	sunny	rains	snows

1 In January it is _____ cold.
2 In February it is _____ hot.
3 In March it is usually _____.
4 In April it often _____.
5 In May it is _____ hot.
6 In June it is often _____.
7 In July it is never _____.
8 In August it is always _____.
9 In September it never _____.
10 In October it is _____ cold.
11 In November it is usually _____.
12 In December it is _____ cold.

9

Test your memory

Look at these pictures carefully. Then turn to page 12 and try to answer the questions. Do NOT look at the questions first!

Revision

Revision

1 What was the boy's name?

2 What time did Mary wake up?

3 Where did the black cat hide?

4 What did Sam's uncle give him?

5 What did the woman buy the little boy?

6 Did the man in the green shirt dig the hole, or the man in the yellow shirt?

7 Did the postman bring Anne a letter or a parcel?

8 What time did Sam leave home?

Revision

9 How much did the aeroplane cost?

10 Who did Sam meet?

11 What did the children see?

12 How much did the boy pay for the book?

13 What did Mary draw?

14 Who opened the window?

15 What did Sam write on the board?

16 Who caught the fish, Sam, John or Mary?

13

Revision

The picnic

Sam	All right. Where are we going to go?
John	To the big park.
Mike	No, the beach.
Sam	There are going to be a lot of people on the beach tomorrow. Let's go to the park.
Mike	All right. How are we going to get there?
Sam	By bus. There is one at nine o'clock.
John	Where are we going to meet?
Sam	At the bus-stop. I'm going to bring some sandwiches. What are you going to bring?
Mike	I'm going to bring some oranges.
John	I'm going to bring something to drink.
Sam	What are we going to do there?
John	I'm going to bring my radio.
Mike	I'm going to bring my kite.
Sam	I'm going to bring a book.

What are they saying? Can you finish it?

Tomorrow's a holiday, Sam. What are you going to do?

I'm _____ _____ have a picnic.

That's nice. Where are you _____ _____ go?

To the big park.

Who is _____ _____ go with you?

John and Mike.

Can I come?

Yes.

How . . .

By bus.

Where . . .

At the bus-stop.

. . . ?

At nine o'clock.

What are you going to bring?

I'm going to bring some sandwiches.
Mike's . . .
John's . . .
What are you going to bring?

. . . some biscuits.

Good. I'm going to bring a book.
John's . . .
Mike's . . .
What . . . ?

I'm not . . . anything.

15

Revision

Who is doing it?

In the picture on page 16:

Mrs. Clark is wearing a red dress.

Peter Clark has a yellow shirt.

Mrs. Jones is wearing a green dress.

Susan Jones is wearing a red dress and Alan Jones is wearing a black and white shirt.

Tom Lee is wearing a red and white shirt and Mary is wearing a white dress.

Dick's shirt is white.

Brian Lee's car is yellow and black.

Mr. Ford is an old man with a stick.

Mr. Clark is wearing a white hat.

Suzy Clark is wearing a green and yellow dress.

Danny Clark has a green shirt.

Make sentences about the picture.

Mrs. Clark		saying, 'Don't be greedy'.
Peter Clark		running across the road carelessly.
Mrs. Jones		riding carelessly.
Susan Jones		talking noisily.
Alan Jones		shouting angrily.
Tom	is	saying, 'Be careful!'
Mary		buying Suzy a kite.
Dick		driving dangerously.
Brian Lee		saying, 'Please be quiet!'
Mr. Ford		buying Danny an aeroplane.
Mr. Clark		eating greedily.

Which picture fits the sentence?

A

The girl in the boat is catching a crab.

B

The boy on the rock is combing his hair.

C

The man with the umbrella is getting into a taxi.

D

The boy with the aeroplane is wearing black shoes.

E

The girl with long hair is carrying a doll with red shoes.

F

My brother is the one in the shorts without a tie.

G

The man in the white coat put some petrol into the car with the red roof.

H

The dog with black spots was asleep under the tree.

I *Which picture fits the conversation?*

Mrs. Clark	How much is the dress with the yellow collar?
Shopkeeper	It's 200.
Mrs. Clark	That's too expensive.
Shopkeeper	The one with the red collar is only 150.
Mrs. Clark	No, thank you. I want one with short sleeves. That one's got long sleeves.

J *Which man is John talking about?*

John	Look at the funny man.
Sam	Which one?
John	The one with the basket.
Sam	There are two men with a basket. Which one?
John	The one with glasses.
Sam	Oh, yes, I see him. Why is he funny?
John	He's wearing only one sock!

K *Which picture are they looking at?*

| 1 | 2 | 3 | 4 |

Sam   I drew that picture.
John Which one?
Sam   The one of the tiger in a cage. Do you like it?
John Not much.
Sam   Why not?
John The tiger's tail is too short.

L *Which watch does Annie like?*

| A | B | C |

Kate   Which watch do you like Annie?
Annie I'm not sure. I don't like the one on the left.
Kate   Why not?
Annie I don't like watches with hands. I like numbers.
Kate   I like the one in the middle. Do you?
Annie No, I like watches with the time and the date.
Kate   You like that one, do you?
Annie That's right, but it's too expensive for me!

What's the difference?

1

2

How many differences did you see in the pictures on page 22? Here is one:

In the first picture, the woman in the red dress is carrying a bag.
In the second picture, the woman in the red dress is carrying a basket.

Here are some words you can use:

carrying a parcel/carrying a letter
has red shoes/has green shoes
getting into a car/getting into a taxi
reading a newspaper/reading a book
eating an ice-cream/eating an apple
combing her hair/writing in a book
riding a bicycle/walking with a bicycle
looking into a shop window/not looking into a shop window

Say and spell:

1   get, gate   tick, take   wet, wait   kick, cake

2

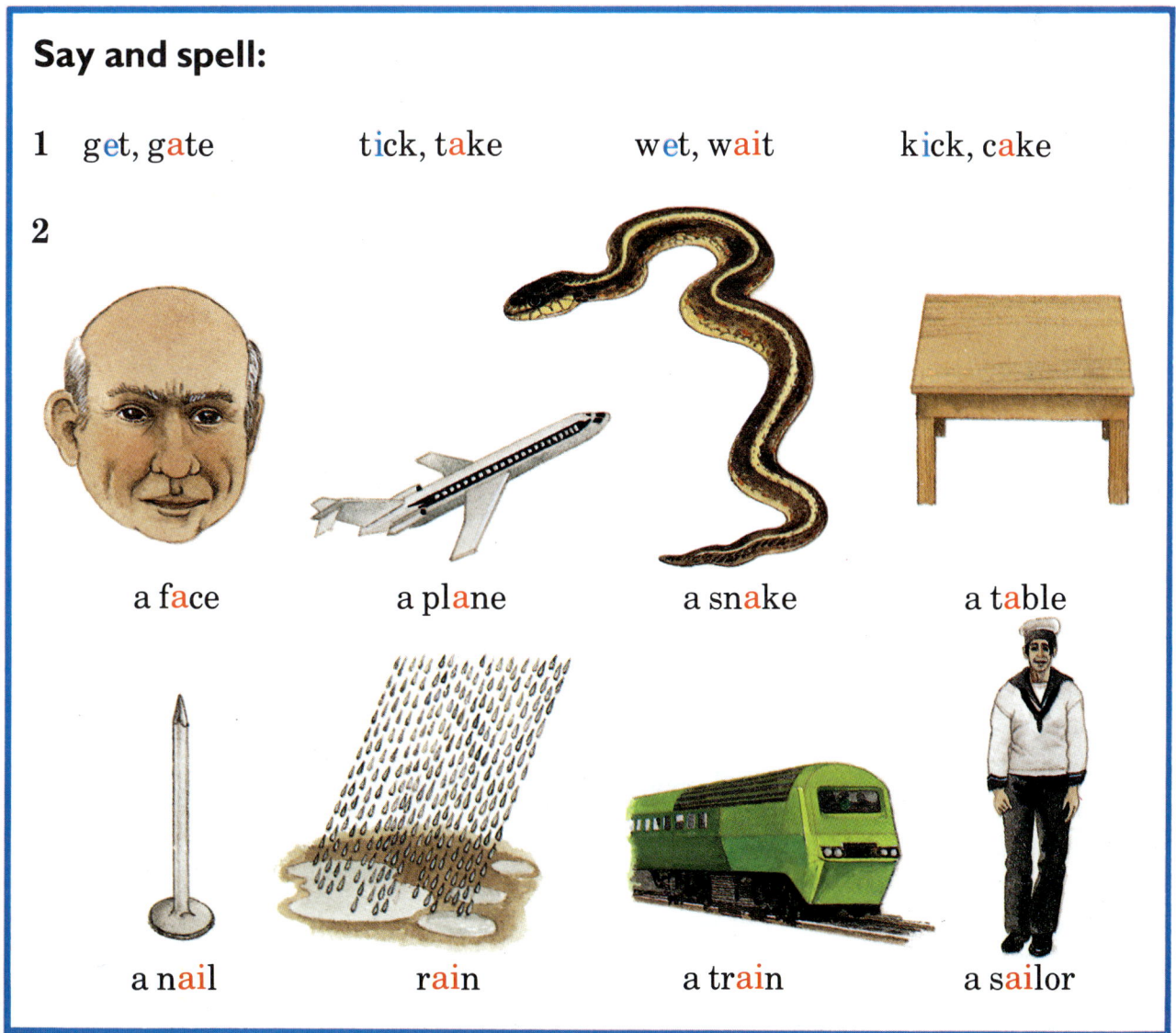

a face   a plane   a snake   a table

a nail   rain   a train   a sailor

What's a–?

A   What's a belt?
B   This is a belt.
A   Yes, you're right. That's a belt.

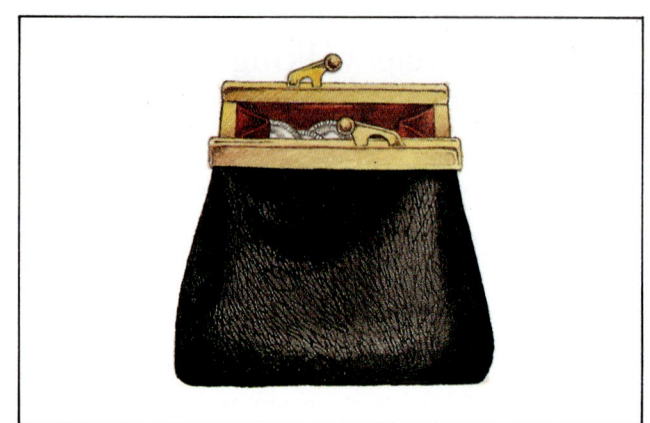

A   What's a wallet?
B   I think this is a wallet.
A   No, that's wrong. It's a purse.

A   What's a teapot?
B   I'm not sure. I think number 18 is a teapot. Am I right?
A   I don't know.

Ask your friend questions about these.
They are all on the next page.

a hammer	a ladder	a lorry	a tie
a triangle	an ant	a magnet	a sailor
a lamp	a tent	a star	a bed
a typewriter	a tick	a puzzle	a calendar
an iron	a rabbit	a teapot	a needle
a parcel	a dentist	a photograph	a guitar

How do you spell–?

Ask your friend how to spell these things.
(The answers are on the next page.)

A How do you spell 'Bicycle'?
B B–Y–B–I–C–L–E.
A No, that's wrong. Try again.
B B–I–C–Y–C–L–E.
A Correct! Well done!

1	2	3
4	5	6
7	8	9
10	11	12
13	14	15

A clever trick

Sam   I'm sure you can't spell three easy words.

John   Yes, I can. I'm good at spelling. Let me try.

Sam   All right. Are you ready?

John   Yes, I'm ready. Begin.

Sam   Orange.

John   O–R–A–N–G–E.

Sam   Apple.

John   A–P–P–L–E.

Sam   Wrong.

John   Wrong? Is it? Let me try again.
A–P–L–E.

Sam   Wrong.

John   Yes, it has two Ps. A–P–P–L–E.

Sam   Wrong.

John   Then I don't know.

Sam   You failed! You didn't spell the three
words. You didn't spell the third word. The
third word was 'wrong'. W–R–O–N–G!

John   That was a trick.

Sam   Yes, it tricked you!

Spelling answers

1 shoe	2 bread	3 aeroplane	4 basket	5 boat
6 clothes	7 cupboard	8 eye	9 ceiling	10 flower
11 piano	12 fruit	13 biscuit	14 leaf	15 ice-cream

What does it mean?

A   What does the word 'mountain' mean?
B   It's a very big hill.
A   I see. Thank you. What does 'narrow' mean?
B   It means 'not wide'.

*Ask your friend what these words mean. The
answers are in the wrong order.*

1	beautiful	a.	a place where you buy things
2	people	b.	the top of your arm
3	shop	c.	very pretty
4	cheap	d.	an animal which lives in water
5	shoulder	e.	men, women, boys and girls
6	fish	f.	anything you eat
7	elephant	g.	the first meal of the day
8	food	h.	not expensive
9	breakfast	i.	chairs, tables, cupboards and other things
10	doctor	j.	behaving badly
11	furniture	k.	a person who looks after sick people
12	naughty	l.	a very big animal

Say and spell:

1   bag, beg   pan, pen   bad, bed   man, men

2

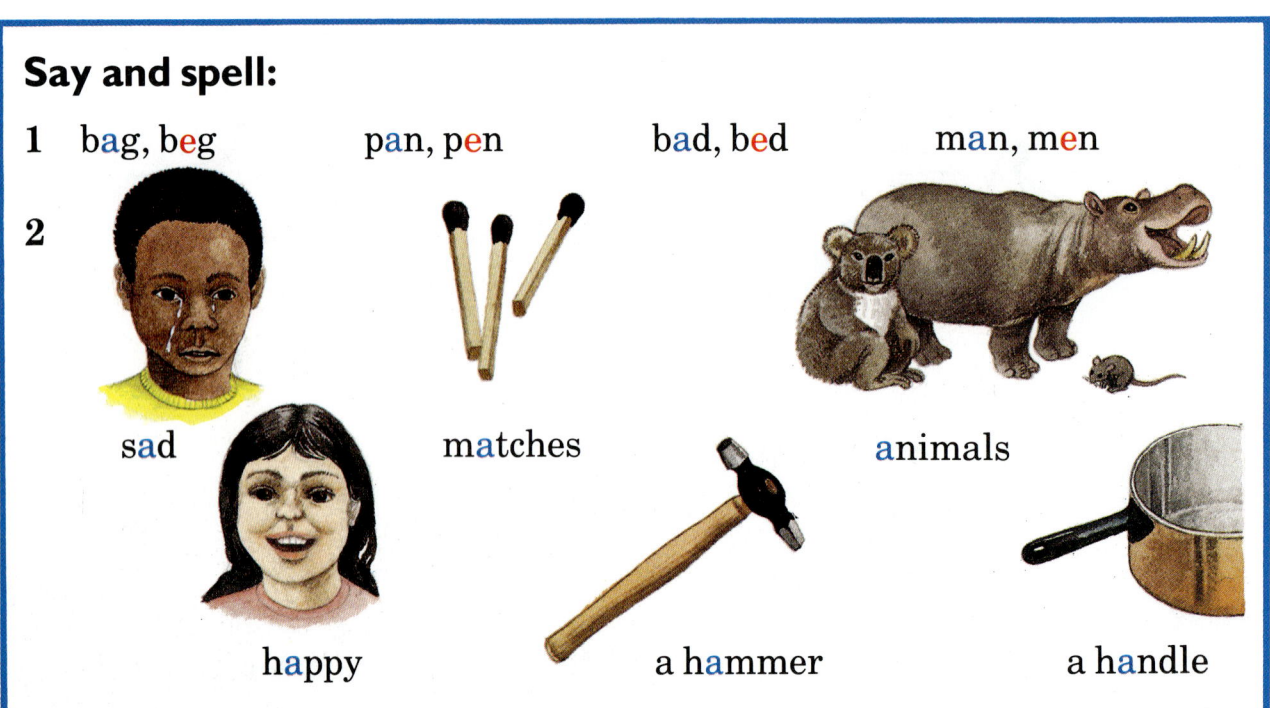

sad   matches   animals

happy   a hammer   a handle

UNIT 3 Problems

Read and answer the questions.

This is a magnet.
Iron things stick to it.
We call one end the North Pole.
We call the other end the South Pole.

North Pole   South Pole

north   south

This is a magnet, too.
It is a bar magnet.
It is a different shape but it is a magnet.
In the drawing it is hanging from a piece of string.
One end, the North Pole, always points to the north.
The other end always points to the south.
It is a compass.

This is a compass, too.
Look at the needle.
It is pointing to the north.
A compass needle always points to the north.
Look at the letters.
We call these the points of the compass.

N = north   S = south
E = east   W = west

29

1 Does a pin stick to a magnet?
2 Does a nail stick to a magnet?
3 Does a pencil stick to a magnet?

4 Is a magnet always a U shape?
5 What do we call a magnet with this shape?

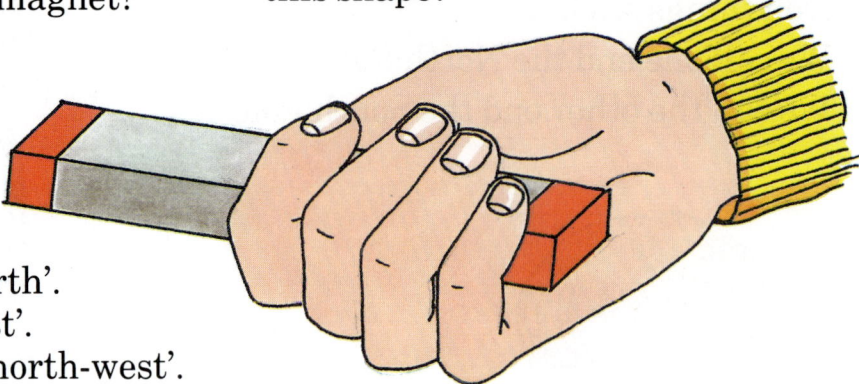

6 The letter N means 'north'.
The letter E means 'east'.
The letters NW mean 'north-west'.
What do these letters mean?
a. NE   **b.** SW   **c.** SE

Read and answer the questions.

This is the world.
Can you see the points of the compass?
Can you see the aeroplane?
Where is it travelling?
It is going north.
Can you see the ship? Where is it going?
It is travelling east.

The world

There is a compass in the aeroplane.
The needle is pointing to the north.
There is a compass in the ship.
The needle is pointing to the north.
Every aeroplane has a compass.
Every ship has a compass.
A compass on a ship or an aeroplane is very important.
It tells the captain his direction.
It tells him where to go.

Walkers sometimes use compasses.
They look at a map.
They decide their direction.
Then they look at a compass.
Then they point.
'That is our direction', they say.

1 Look at the drawing of the world on page 30.
  What is the direction of the ship?
  Its direction is . . .

2 What is the direction of the aeroplane?

3 Where can we always find a compass?

4 Why is a compass very important on a ship or an
  aeroplane?
  It tells the captain . . .

5 You are facing north. You turn left. Where are
  you facing now?

6 You are facing north. You turn right. Where are
  you facing now?

7 You are facing south. You turn left. Where are
  you facing now?

8 Four men started to walk. They all walked
  south but they all walked in different
  directions. After a long time they met again.
  Where did they start walking?

Which?

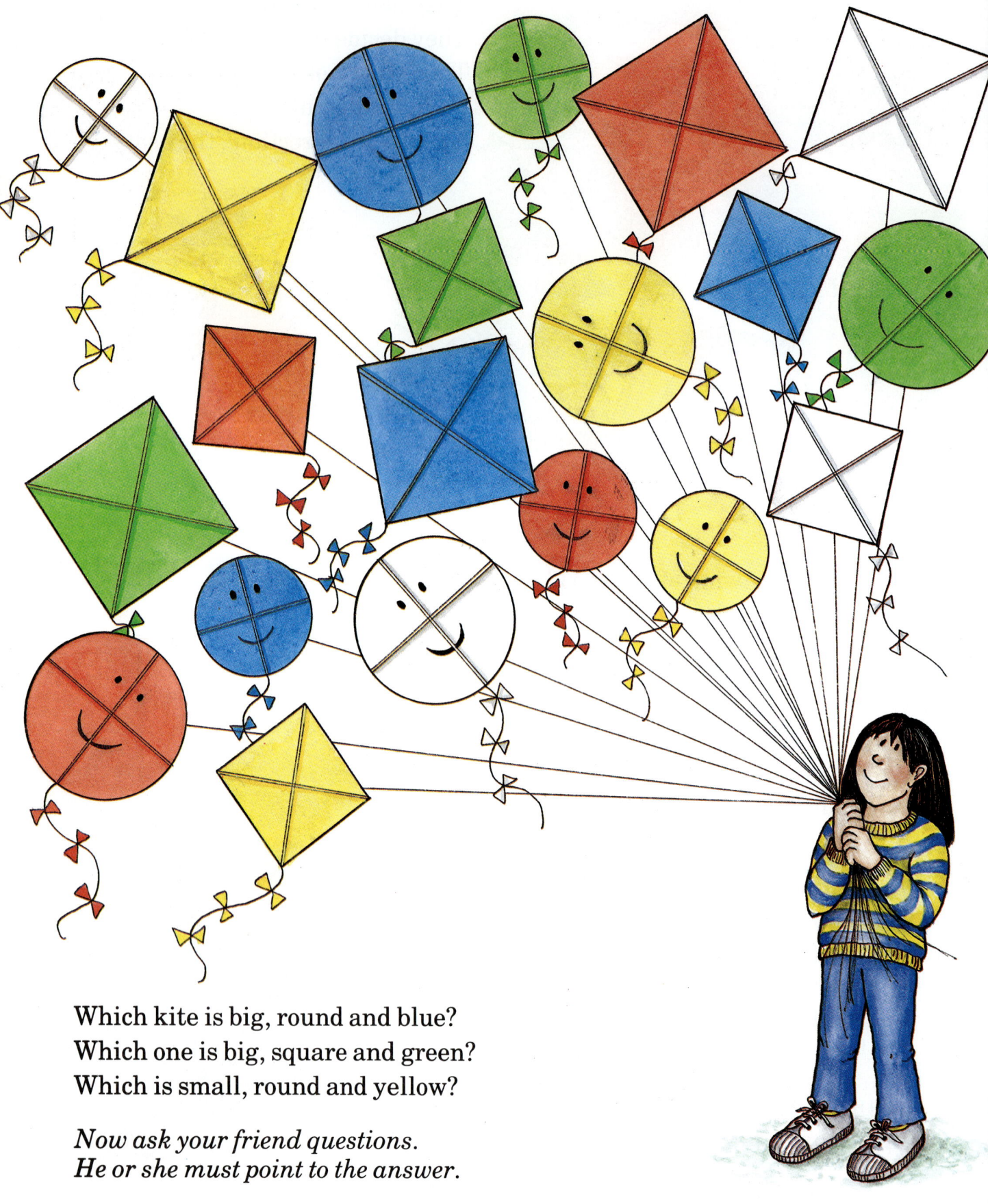

Which kite is big, round and blue?
Which one is big, square and green?
Which is small, round and yellow?

Now ask your friend questions.
He or she must point to the answer.

How much?

Sam's mother sent him to the shop.

Sam bought:

some bread.	The bread cost 2.50.
some jam.	The jam cost 4.00.
some coffee.	The coffee cost 6.50.
some sugar.	The sugar cost 5.50.
some ice-cream.	The ice-cream cost 1.50.
some tea.	The tea cost 2.00.

1 How much did Sam spend? £22.00

2 He gave the shopkeeper three ten coins.
   How much did the shopkeeper give Sam? £8.00

3 The following week Sam went again. This time
   the ice-cream was more expensive. Sam gave
   the shopkeeper twenty-three. How much did the
   ice-cream cost? £2.50

4 The following week the bread was more
   expensive. It cost three-fifty. Sam gave
   the shopkeeper fifty. How much did the
   shopkeeper give Sam? £46.50

Now ask your friend some questions.

Who?

1A   1B   1C   1D   1E   1F

Sam   Susan   John   Mary   Mike   Sarah

Six children went to the cinema. They saw a film about wild animals. They sat in a row. Their seats were numbered **1A, 1B, 1C, 1D, 1E** and **1F**.

Mike did not sit next to John. He sat next to Sarah.

Susan sat between Sam and John.

Sam sat in 1A.

Mary sat on the left of Mike.

Which seats did they sit in? Write down the seat numbers and the children's names on a piece of paper.

1   Who sat between John and Mike? *Mary*
2   Sam sat at one end of the row. Who sat at the other end? *Sarah*
3   Who sat next to Sam? *Susan*
4   Who sat on the right of Susan? *John*
5   Where did Mike sit? *bet. Mary + Sarah*

Now ask your friend some questions like those above.

34

When?

Mr. Lee

Mr. Lee's 21st birthday was in 1973.
He started school at the age of six and left when he was eighteen.
He married at the age of twenty-five.

Mr. Taylor

Mr. Taylor is two years older than Mr. Lee. He started school at the age of six. He left when he was sixteen.
He married at the age of twenty-three.

Mr. Clark

Mr. Clark is three years younger than Mr. Lee.
He started school at the age of six and left when he was nineteen.
He married seven years later.

Write the answers on a piece of paper.

		Mr. T.	Mr. C
1 When was Mr. Lee born?	In 1952.	In 1950.	In 1955.
2 When did he start school?	In 1958	In 1956.	In 1961.
3 When did he leave school?	In 1970	In 1968.	In 1974
4 When did he marry?	In 1977	In 1973.	In 1981

Now ask your friend questions about Mr. Taylor and Mr. Clark.

What are they saying? Use the sentences on page 37.

open the window

close the window

open the door

tell me your name / sit there

help us to carry it

lend me a pen

direct me to the ferry / move your car

tell me your name

post this letter

switch on the light

Will		pass the pepper,	
		direct me to the ferry,	
		take me to the City Hall,	
		turn off the radio,	
		lend me a pen,	
		close the window,	
		sit there,	
	you	open the window,	please?
		help us to carry it,	
		tell me your name,	
Would		open the door,	
		move your car,	
		post this letter for me,	
		switch on the light,	
		lend me some money,	
		repeat that,	

Mr. Clark hangs a picture

'Will you hang this picture on the wall, please?' said Mrs. Clark. 'Would you put it in the centre, please?'

'Certainly,' said Mr. Clark. 'That's a very easy job. I can do that easily. David, will you please go to Mr. Ford in the next flat? Borrow a ladder from him. Don't forget to say "please". Tom, will you go to the shop, please, and buy some wire. Will you buy some small screws, too, please? Now, where's that ladder?'

'Here it is, father,' said David. 'Mr. Ford wants it back tomorrow.'

'Thank you,' said Mr. Clark. 'Would you get a ruler, please, Anne? I want to measure the wall.'

'Yes, father,' said Anne.

'Now, David,' said Mr. Clark. 'Will you please go to Mr. Ford again. Will you ask him to lend me his hammer, please? Be quick.'

'Yes, father,' said David.

'Hello, Tom. Where are the screws and the wire?'

'Here they are, father,' said Tom.

'Good! Now will you please put two screws into the back of the picture? Then cut a piece of wire and join the wire to them. Can you do that?'

'Yes, father,' said Tom.

'Anne, would you please measure the wall and find the centre?'

'Yes, father. Here it is.'

'Here is the hammer, father,' said David.

'Good!' said Mr. Clark. 'Here is a nail. Climb up and hammer the nail into the wall. Tom, will you hold the ladder, please? That's right. Good! Well done, David. Will you give him the picture, please, Anne? Hang it straight, David. That's right. Good! That's very good!'

'Thank you, father,' said David.

'Would you please take the hammer and the ladder back to Mr. Ford? Anne, would you please ask your mother to come in?'

'Thank you,' said Mrs. Clark. 'It looks very nice.'

'It was an easy job,' said Mr. Clark. 'I did it very quickly.'

Choose the right answer.

1 Mrs. Clark wanted the picture to be

   a. in the middle of the wall.
   b. on the right side of the wall.
   c. at the top of the wall.
   d. at the bottom of the wall.

2 David went to Mr. Ford's flat to borrow

   a. a ladder and some screws.
   b. some wire and some screws.
   c. a ruler and some wire.
   d. a ladder and a hammer.

3 Who brought the ruler?

   a. David.
   b. Anne.
   c. Tom.
   d. Mrs. Clark.

4 Mr. Clark asked Tom to

   a. put a nail in the wall.
   b. put two screws in the wall.
   c. put a nail in the picture.
   d. put two screws in the picture.

5 Who hammered the nail into the wall?

   a. Tom.
   b. Anne.
   c. Mr. Clark.
   d. David.

6 Who did all the work?

   a. Mr. Clark.
   b. Mrs. Clark.
   c. David.
   d. The children.

A game

Now play the game with one pencil and one pen.

B May I have the pencil, please?   **A** Here it is.   **B** Thank you.

Say and spell:

1   p**o**t, p**ar**t   sh**o**p, sh**ar**p

2

a f**ar**mer   a p**ar**cel   a c**ar**   a gl**a**ss   gl**a**sses

gr**a**ss   a h**a**lf   a p**a**th   a st**ar**   l**au**ghing

41

UNIT 5 What would they like?

A puzzle

(Your teacher will tell you the answer to this puzzle.)

Mr. Wood would not like these things. Why not?		Mr. Wood would like these things. Why?	
a shoe	a fork	a boot	a spoon
a pear	some tea	an apple	some coffee
a dog	a cat	a puppy	a kitten
a comb	a pencil	a toothbrush	a rubber

Would you like some jam, Mr. Wood? — No, thank you, but I'd like some butter.

Would you like a newspaper, Mr. Wood? — No, thank you, but I'd like a book.

Would you like a glass, Mr. Wood? — Yes, please. I'd like a glass.

Would you like some eggs, Mr. Wood? — Yes, please. I'd like some eggs.

42

Mr. Green would not like these things. Why not?	Mr. Green would rather have these things. Why?
 a cake	a sweet
some salt	 some pepper
 a duck	a rabbit
a tin	 a glass
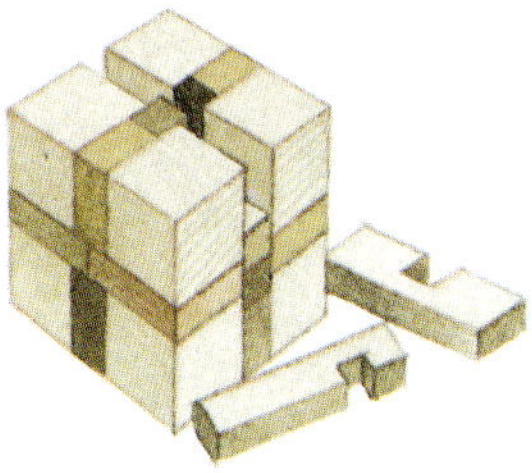 a game	a puzzle
a bowl	 a bottle
 some water	some food
a drum	 a bell

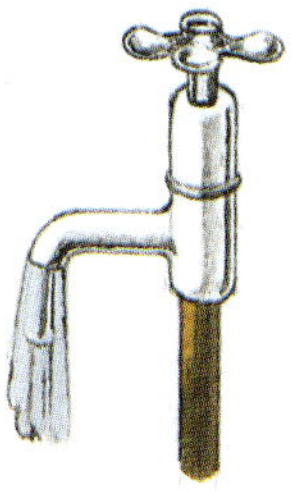

Would you like a cow, Mr. Green?　　　　No, thank you. I'd rather have a sheep.
Would you like a cake, Mr. Green?　　　 No, thank you. I'd rather have a sweet.
Would you like a ball, Mr. Green?　　　　Yes, please. I'd like a ball.
Would you like some wood, Mr. Green?　Yes, please. I'd like some wood.

Some rhymes to read or learn

'Would you like some orange juice?
    I'm giving it a squeeze.
Would you like a nice long drink?'
    'Oh, yes, please!'

'Would you like a hamburger?
    It looks very good.
Would you like some sandwiches?'
    'Yes, I would!'

'Would you like some vegetables?
    Would you like some peas?
Would you like some tomatoes?'
    'Oh, yes, please!'

'Would you like some coffee?
    Would you like some tea?
Who would like some ice-cream?'
    'Me! Me! Me!'

'Would you like a pineapple?
    Would you like two?
Would you like a lot of them?'
    'Yes, please. Wouldn't you?'

'Would you like some medicine?
    It can make you grow.
Would you like a spoonful?'
    'No, no, no!'

'Would you like a holiday?
    There's one very near.
Would you like a long one?'
    'Yes, about a year!'

'Would you like a goldfish?
  It isn't very old.
I think it's very beautiful.'
  'I'd rather have some gold!'

'A rabbit is a pretty pet.
  Would you like a frog?
Would you like an elephant?'
  'I'd rather have a dog!'

'Would you like to play with me?
  You can fly my kite.
You can ride my bicycle.'
  'Oh, all right!'

'Would you like to climb that hill?
  Would you like to walk?
Would you like to run with me?'
  'Thanks. I'd rather talk!'

'Would you like to go by bus?
  Would you like a car?
Would you like to go on foot?'
  'No, thanks. It's much too far!'

'It's time to do your homework.
  Would you like some ink?
Would you like some paper?'
  'I'd rather have a drink!'

'Would you like a candle?
  Would you like a light?
Would you like to do some work?'
  'No, thanks. Good night!'

The king and the mice

A king once lived in a far-off country. He lived in a beautiful palace. He had lots of everything: money, jewels, fine clothes – and lots of cheese. He liked cheese very much.

'I would rather have cheese than any other food,' he said. 'Bring me more cheese!' His cooks made him many different kinds of cheese. The king ate them all.

There was one problem. Mice like cheese, too, and the palace was full of mice. There were mice everywhere. The king sent for his wise men. 'Send these mice away,' he said. 'I don't like them. They are eating my cheese.'

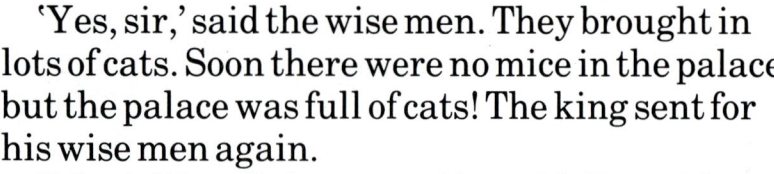

'Yes, sir,' said the wise men. They brought in lots of cats. Soon there were no mice in the palace but the palace was full of cats! The king sent for his wise men again.

'I don't like all these cats,' he said. 'I would rather have mice! Send these cats away.'

'Yes, sir,' said the wise men. 'We can do that easily.' They brought in dogs. There were black dogs, white dogs, big dogs and little dogs. Soon the palace was full of dogs, and all the cats went away. The dogs were very happy in the palace but the king was not.

'I don't like all these dogs,' he said. 'I would rather have cats! Make the dogs go away, please.'

'Yes, sir,' said the wise men. 'We can easily do that.'

They brought in lions! The palace was full of lions. They were big, strong lions and soon all the dogs left the palace. But the king was very unhappy.

'I don't like all these lions,' he said. 'I'm afraid of them. I would rather have dogs! Will you please make the lions go away?'

'Yes, sir,' said the wise men, and they filled the palace with elephants! Lions are afraid of elephants and they quickly went away.

The king was very unhappy. 'I can't have elephants in my palace,' he said. I would rather have lions! Make them go away!'

'Yes,' said the wise men, and they brought back the mice. Elephants hate mice and soon there were no elephants in the palace – but the palace was full of mice again.

'All right,' said the king. 'The mice can stay. They can have some of my cheese, but not too much. Then we will all be happy.'

Put these sentences in the right order:

He ate a lot of cheese.
The wise men brought cats and the mice went away.
Lions made the dogs go away.
The palace was full of mice.
The wise men brought back the mice and the elephants left.
The wise men brought dogs and the cats went away.
A rich king lived in a beautiful palace.
The king let the mice stay in the palace.
Elephants made the lions go away.
The king told his wise men to send the mice away.

UNIT 6 What will happen?

This is Tom's timetable for tomorrow.

Tom

Anna goes to a different school.
This is her timetable for tomorrow.

Anna

6.30	Get up
7.00	Have breakfast
7.45	Arrive at school
8.00	Go into the school hall
8.15	First lesson: Science
9.00	Geography
9.45	History
10.30	Break
11.00	English
11.45	Mathematics
12.30	Lunch
1.30	Games
3.00	Go home
4.30	Homework
9.30	Go to bed

6.45	Get up
7.15	Have breakfast
8.00	Arrive at school
8.10	First lesson: English
8.50	Mathematics
9.30	Science
11.00	Break
11.20	Geography
11.50	English
12.30	Lunch
1.30	History
2.10	Games
4.00	Go home
5.00	Homework
9.45	Go to bed

Tomorrow Tom will get up a half past six. He will have breakfast at seven and arrive at school at a quarter to eight. He will go into the school hall at eight and the first lesson, Science, will begin at eight fifteen.

The second lesson, Geography, will begin at nine and a History lesson will begin at nine forty-five.

Tom will have a break at ten thirty. Then he will have a Mathematics lesson at a quarter to twelve. He will have lunch at half past twelve. There will be games at one thirty and he will go home at three. He will do his homework at half past four and he will go to bed at nine thirty.

What will Anna do tomorrow?

48

Who is saying what?

Don't touch that dog. It'll bite you.

Don't run across the road. You'll be killed.

Be careful with that knife. You'll cut somebody.

Don't eat that third ice-cream. You'll be sick.

Get off that fence. You'll fall down.

Don't fly it that way. You'll lose it.

Put out the light. You'll be tired in the morning.

Don't be silly. You'll fall off the bicycle.

Mr. Slack's egg

Mr. Slack was a lazy man. He did not like to work. He would rather sit in the sun and dream.

One day he went for a walk in the country. He stopped for a rest and sat down under a tree. Then he saw a hen's egg lying on the grass under the tree.

'An egg!' he thought. 'I am very lucky. This will make me rich.'

Just then a friend saw him.

'Hello, Mr. Slack,' he said. 'What have you got in your hand?'

'An egg!' said Mr. Slack. 'I'm very lucky, aren't I?'

'An egg?' said his friend. 'Is that all?'

'You don't understand,' said Mr. Slack. 'This egg will make me rich.'

His friend laughed. 'Please explain,' he said.

'Listen to me,' said Mr. Slack. 'I shall not eat this egg. I shall put it in my pocket. It will be warm there. Soon a chicken will come out of the egg. The chicken will grow into a hen. The hen will lay eggs. Those eggs will give me more chickens. They will grow into hens. Those hens will lay eggs. Soon I shall have hundreds of hens and eggs. I shall sell them and I shall be a rich man. I shall live in a big house and I shall have lots of servants. I shall have four cars with men to drive them. I shall be a very important man. People will point at me and say, "Look! That's Mr. Slack. He's a very rich man." Then I shall . . . .'

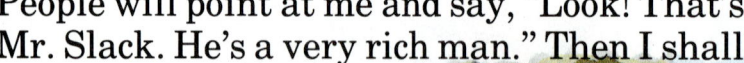

'Stop!' said his friend. You're going too fast. Let me look at this wonderful egg.'

Mr. Slack took the egg out of his pocket to show his friend but it slipped from his fingers.

Mr. Slack looked at the broken egg. 'Oh dear!' he said. 'Now I shall not have any chickens. I shall not have any hens. They will not lay any eggs. I shall not be rich. I shall not have a big house. I shall not have lots of servants or four cars. Oh dear!'

'Yes,' said his friend. 'You will always be poor, Mr. Slack, but perhaps you will be happier. Rich people are often unhappy, you know.'

'Perhaps you're right,' said Mr. Slack sadly.

Choose the best answer.

1 Mr. Slack was a
    a. hard-working
    b. clever   man.
    c. foolish

2 Mr. Slack saw an egg
    a. in the sun.
    b. under the tree.
    c. in the tree.

3 Mr. Slack decided to
    a. keep the egg in his pocket.
    b. put the egg in the sun.
    c. eat the egg.

4 Mr. Slack wanted to have four
    a. houses.
    b. servants.
    c. cars.

5 Mr. Slack wanted to be
    a. lucky.
    b. rich.
    c. clever.

6 Mr. Slack's friend thought that he would always be
    a. unhappy.
    b. rich.
    c. poor.

Sam's trick

Sam's secret

The answer will **always** be 198! Try it. Write any three numbers. Remember: they must be following numbers. Subtract the smaller number from the bigger number. The answer will always be 198!

432	543	765	987
− 234	− 345	− 567	− 789
198	198	198	198

Try Sam's trick on your friend!

Another of Sam's tricks

Sam Try this trick.
You'll like it.
Think of a number.

Sam Multiply by three.

Sam Add one.

Sam Multiply by three.

Sam Add your first number.

Sam Good! Now I can't tell you the number but I can tell you the last number. It's three. Now tell me the number.

Sam Right. The number you first thought of was five.

Sam That's my secret!

John All right!

John Yes.

John Yes.

John All right!

John Yes.

John 53.

John That's right. How do you know?

$5 \times 3 = 15$
$15 + 1 = 16$
$16 \times 3 = 48$
$48 + 5 = 53$

Sam's secret: The last number will always be three. The other number will always be the first number. Try it!

53

Note

We write:	*We say:*
I shall *or* I will	I'll
We shall *or* We will	We'll
He will	He'll
She will	She'll
It will	It'll
They will	They'll
You will	You'll

Read aloud: I'll, he'll, she'll, you'll, we'll, it'll, they'll, she'll, I'll, he'll, we'll, it'll, you'll, they'll

We write:	*We say:*
I shall not *or* I will not	I shan't *or* I won't
We shall not *or*	We shan't *or* We won't
We will not	
He will not	He won't
She will not	She won't
It will not	It won't
They will not	They won't
You will not	You won't

Say and spell:

1

e he she we these Chinese

ee see three free knee kneel deep sweet sheet week asleep greedy

ea sea seat tea teapot teacher easy please speak meal steal leaf cheap cheaply meat ice-cream

ie piece chief fierce fiercely

2

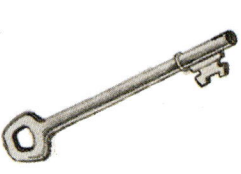
a key

people

a policeman

the ceiling

All English children learn this rhyme. It is very old.

Old Mother Hubbard

Old Mother Hubbard
Went to the cupboard
To get her poor dog a bone,
But when she got there
The cupboard was bare*
And so the poor dog had none.

She went to the baker's
To buy him some bread,
But when she came back
He stood on his head!

She went to the fruit shop
To buy him some fruit,
But when she came back
He was playing the flute!

She went to the tailor's
To buy him a coat,
But when she came back
He was riding a goat!

She went to the shoe shop
To buy him some shoes,
But when she came back
He was reading the news!

She went to the hat shop
To buy him a hat,
But when she came back
He was feeding the cat!

She went to the flower shop
To buy him a rose,
But when she came back
He was dressed in his clothes!

* empty

A *Where did they go? Why?*

1 Mary
to see the animals

2 Tom
to get some medicine

3 Mrs. Clark
to buy some fish

4 Sarah
to have a swim

5 Mr. Clark
to get a book

6 Susan
to see her aunt

7 John
to buy a kite

8 The children
to see a film

Mary went to the zoo to see the animals.

B *What did they do? Why?*

David switched on the radio		make a dress.
Anne bought some cloth		hear some music.
Sam went to the shop	to	buy some clothes.
Mr. Jones bought a newspaper		send to her aunt.
Sarah bought a postcard		read the news.

David switched on the radio to hear some music.

A treasure hunt

One of these men will give you something nice. Which man?
Follow the clues. Start with Mr. Taylor.

A *We use scissors to cut paper. What do we do with the other things on page 57?*

B *Pretend that you are a mother or father, with a lot of children. They are all asking for things. What will you say to them? The pictures will help you to find things to give them.*

I haven't anything to read.

Here's a book for you to read.

I'd like some money to spend.

Here's two-fifty for you to spend.

a saucer of milk

a pencil

a pen

a paintbrush

a biscuit

a ball

1 I haven't anything to eat.
2 I'd like something to drink.
3 Will you give me something to play with, please?
4 I haven't anything to write with.
5 I haven't anything to paint with.
6 I haven't anything to draw with.
7 My dog hasn't anything to eat.
8 My cat hasn't anything to drink.

a bone

a glass of milk

A visit to the zoo

Tomorrow the children are going to the zoo to see the animals. They are going to the monkey-house to see the monkeys, and to the lion-house to see the lions. Sam and John are going to the snake-house to see the snakes. Mary and Anne are going to the bird-house.

'John can take something to eat and Sam can take something to drink,' said Mrs. Lee. 'I'll give Mary some money to spend.'

'I shall take some biscuits for the monkeys to eat,' said Anne.

1 Who will see the monkeys?
2 Who will see the lions?
3 Who will see the snakes?
4 Who will see the birds?

5 What will John take?
6 What will Sam take?
7 What will Mary take?
8 What will Anne take?

Say and spell:

1   eat, it   leaf, live   sheep, ship   wheel, will
    seat, sit   these, this   reach, rich   heat, hit

2   drink   children   happily   history   holiday
    dinner   easily   foolishly   little   middle
    film   fisherman   listen   milk   kitchen
    kitten   lift   picture   different
    multiply   notice-board English   family

Some puzzles

A Some of these trees are big.
Some of them are small.
Some of them are bigger than some of the others.
Some of them are smaller than some of the others.

Which is the biggest tree?
Which is the smallest tree?

1

2

3

4

5

6

7

8

B Which tree is the tallest? Which is the shortest?
Decide. Then measure.

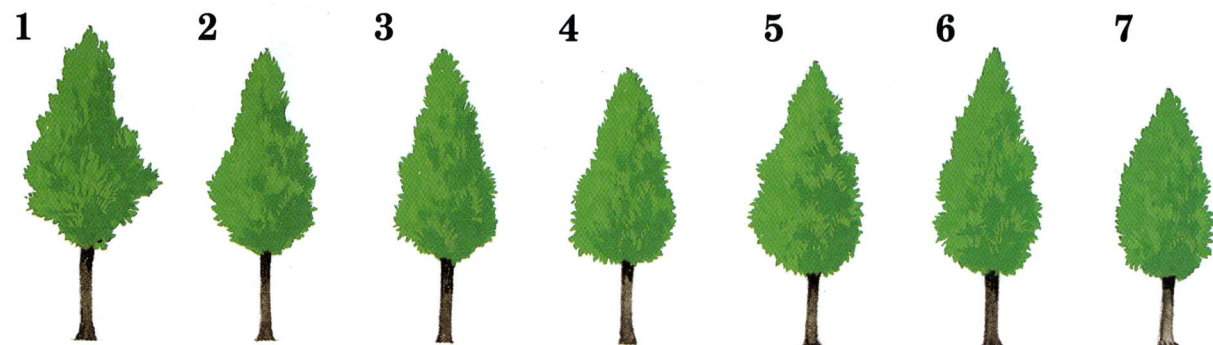

C Which man is the tallest? Which man is the shortest?

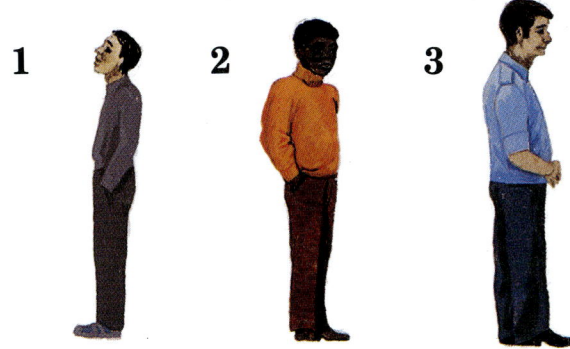

D Which sailor is the tallest?

E Which line is the longest?
Which line is the shortest?

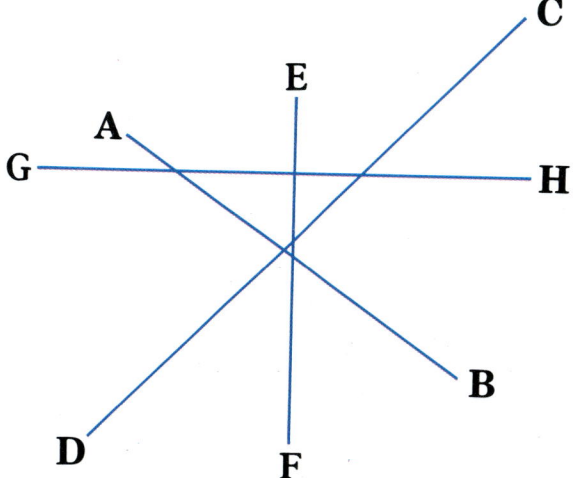

E *Read and answer the questions.*

1

Mr. King	Mr. White	Mr. Ward		Tom	Betty	William

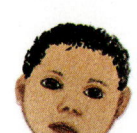

old   older   oldest   young   younger   youngest

Mr. King is old. Mr. White is older.   Tom is young. Betty is younger.
Mr. Ward is the oldest.   William is the youngest.

2

bicycle   car   aeroplane   orange   pear   apple

Which is the slowest?   Which is the most expensive?
Which is the fastest?   Which is the cheapest?

3

girl   man   boy   green shirt yellow shirt white shirt

Who is the happiest?   Which is the cleanest?
Who is the saddest?   Which is the dirtiest?

4

$$2 + 2 \qquad 26 \times 3 \qquad \frac{119}{5} \times \frac{26}{8}$$

Number 1   Number 2   Number 3

Which is the easiest?   Who is the most careful?
Which is the most difficult?   Who is the most careless?

62

F *Do you know?*

1 Which is the biggest ocean in the world?
 a. The Pacific Ocean
 b. The Atlantic Ocean
 c. The Arctic Ocean

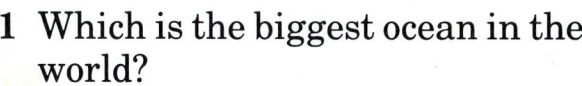

2 Which is the deepest ocean in the world?
 a. The Indian Ocean
 b. The Atlantic Ocean
 c. The Pacific Ocean

3 Which is the highest mountain in the world?
 a. Mount Fuji
 b. Mount Everest
 c. Mount Blanc

4 Which is the largest island in the world?
 a. Greenland
 b. Great Britain
 c. Borneo

5 Which is the longest river in the world?
 a. The Yangtse
 b. The Amazon
 c. The Nile

6 Which is the largest country in the world?
 a. Russia
 b. Brazil
 c. France

7 Which is the fastest animal in the world?
 a. A tiger
 b. A wolf
 c. A cheetah

8 Which is the largest desert in the world?
 a. The Sahara
 b. The Gobi
 c. The Arizona

G *Look at this school report:*

	Sam	John	Susan	Mary
English	A	C	B	D
History	B	A	D	C
Geography	B	C	D	A
Maths	C	B	A	D
Science	C	A	B	D
Music	D	C	B	A

In English Sam was the best and Mary was the worst.

In History John was the best and Susan was the worst.

Now talk about the other subjects.

H *Choose the right words.*

1 Mary is   **a.** younger   **b.** the young   girl in the class.   **c.** the youngest

2 Peter is   **a.** old than   **b.** the oldest   his brother.   **c.** older than

3 Simon is   **a.** biggest   **b.** the bigger   boy in the school.   **c.** the biggest

4 The last exercise was   **a.** difficult   **b.** most difficult   than the others.   **c.** more difficult

5 The boys' marks were
  a. the worst
  b. worse   than the girls'.
  c. worst

6 John's marks were
  a. good
  b. better   in the class.
  c. the best

Say and spell:

1 short
    shorter
    the shortest

long	cheap
tall	clever
brave	wide
weak	young
clean	cold
low	strong
old	new
small	large
thick	narrow

2 big
    bigger
    the biggest

fat
hot
sad
thin

3 happy
    happier
    the happiest

pretty
greedy
busy
heavy
sleepy
hungry
dirty
ugly

4 beautiful
    more beautiful
    the most beautiful

careful
dangerous
careless
exciting
difficult
comfortable

The laziest boy in the world

There were once three boys. Their names were Tom, Dick and Harry but everybody called them Lazy Tom, Lazy Dick and Lazy Harry. They were very lazy. Their friends said to them, 'You are the laziest boys in the world. No one is lazier than you.'

'Yes, we know,' said the boys, and went to sleep!

One day a stranger came to their village. He heard about these boys and wanted to meet them.

'Which of the three boys is the laziest?' he asked.

'I don't know,' a woman said. 'They are all very, very lazy. Look! You can see them now. They are lying in the sun. They are not doing any work. They are not at school. "Which one is the laziest?" you ask. I don't know.'

'I will find out,' said the stranger. 'Watch.' He went up to the three boys and said, 'Good morning.' The boys did not answer.

'I see,' said the man. 'You are certainly very lazy, and rude, too.'

Then he took out some money and offered it to the first boy, Lazy Tom. Lazy Tom sat up, took the money, and lay down again. He did not stand up. He did not say 'Thank you'.

Then the stranger offered some money to the next boy, Lazy Dick. Lazy Dick did not say 'Thank you'. He did not stand up. He did not sit up. He held out his hand and took the money. Then he closed his eyes.

'I think you are the laziest boy,' said the stranger. Then he offered some money to Lazy Harry. Lazy Harry did not move. He did not stand up. He did not sit up. He did not hold out his hand.

'Put it in my pocket,' he said.

'You are certainly the laziest boy,' said the stranger.

Then he spoke to all three boys. 'Stand up!' he said in a loud voice. 'I am an inspector of schools. Go to school at once! I shall speak to your headmaster tomorrow. But first, give me back the money!'

Put one word in each black space.

The friends of Tom, Dick and Harry said to them, 'You are the _____ boys in the world. No one is _____ than you,' but the three boys went to _____! A stranger came to the _____.

'Which of the boys is _____ laziest?' he asked.

'I don't _____,' a woman said. 'They are all _____ lazy.'

The man offered some money to Lazy Tom. He _____ up and took the money but he did not say, '_____ you'.

The man offered some money to Lazy Dick. Dick did not _____ up but he _____ the money.

The man _____ some money to Lazy Harry but Harry did not _____. He was the _____ of the three boys.

Then the stranger said that he was an _____. He made the boys go to _____.

Read.

This glass is full.

This glass is only half full.

This glass is empty.

This shelf is full of books.

This shelf is only half full of books.

This shelf is empty.

What are they saying?

1

I'm sorry, this bus is _____.

2

Don't dive! The swimming pool is _____!

3

Fill it up, please. My car is _____.

4

It rained a lot in August. The reservoir is _____.

5

May I fill your glass? It's only _____.

6

Put some more sand in that lorry. It's only _____.

7

There's no food for you. The cupboard is _____.

8

Are there any people in the flat?

No, it's _____.

9

Put it in the rubbish bin.

I can't. It's _____.

10

Carry this parcel for me, please. My bag is _____.

11

Why didn't that bus stop? It's only _____.

12

There is room for a lot of books. The shelf is only _____.

How good is your memory?

Try to answer the questions without looking at pages 68 and 69.

1 How many people were there in the bus?

   It was full.

2 How much water was there in the swimming pool?
3 How much petrol was there in the car?
4 How much water was there in the reservoir?
5 How much water was there in the woman's glass?
6 How much sand was there in the lorry?
7 How much food was there in the cupboard?
8 How many people were there in the flat?
9 How much rubbish was there in the bin?
10 How many parcels were there in the woman's bag?
11 How many people were there on the bus?
12 How many books were there on the shelf?

How often?

| We have | English
Mathematics
Science
a meal
Music | once
twice
three times
four times
five times | | a | day.

week. |

1 How often do you go to school?
2 How often do you go to the market?
3 How often do you have homework?
4 How often do you play games?
5 How often do you wash your face?

Do you know?

1 How many people are there in your classroom?
2 How many toes are there in your classroom?
3 How tall are you?
4 How high is your classroom door?
5 How old is your father?
6 How far is the nearest police station?
7 How far is the nearest post office?
8 How many centimetres are there in a metre?

How clever are you?

Here are three questions. Be careful. They are trick questions.

1 A man dug a hole in the ground. These are its measurements:

How much earth was there in the hole?

2 There were twenty birds on a tree. A man took a gun and shot one. How many birds were there on the tree?

3 How many eggs can you put into an empty glass?

Who is answering the question?

Sally

How old are you?

Sam

Anne

How often do you have Music?

John

Mr. Taylor

How much is that watch?

Mr. Lee

Mike

How high is Mount Everest?

Mr. Clark

Mr. Fox

How far is the nearest fire station?

Mr. Jones

Linda

How tall are you?

Mary

Mr. Green

How hot does it get in Bermuda?

Mr. Guy

David

How many people are there in New York?

Mr. Green

Sarah

How long is the Amazon?

Mr. Harris

How much rain do they have in England?

Tom

Mr. Swan

Dick

How many lessons do you have on Monday?

Wendy

"It's only two hundred."

Mr Taylor

"Twice a week."

Anne

"8,848 metres."

Mike

"I'm ten."

Sally

"1.5 metres."

Linda

"About two kilometres."

Mr. Fox

"About 75 centimetres a year."

Tom

"About seven million."

David

"About 6,400 kilometres."

Sarah

"Eight."

Dick

"Thirty-four degrees centigrade."

Mr. Green

How do I get there?

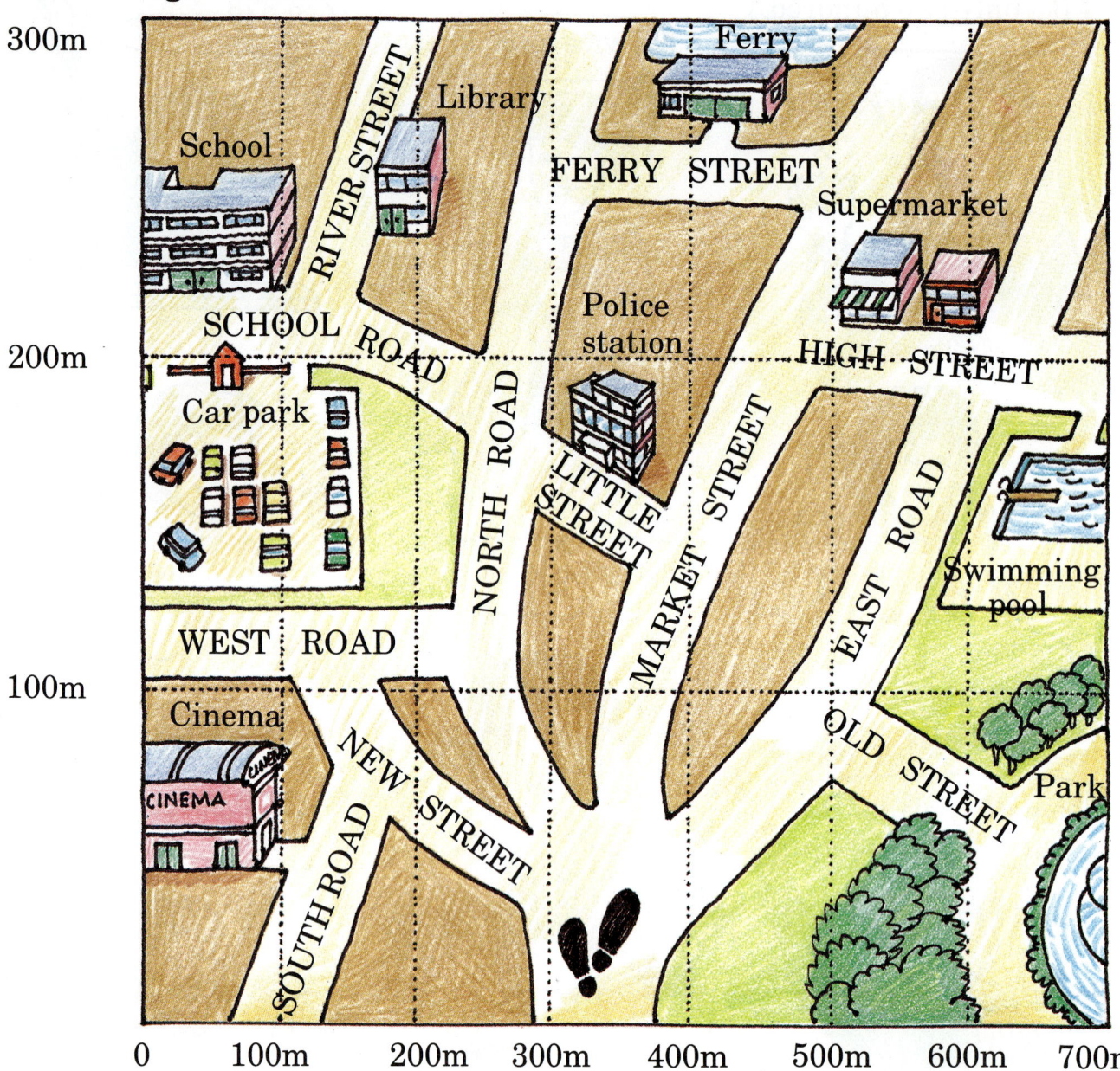

Read.

Mr. A Excuse me. How do I get to the cinema, please?
Mr. B Go along New Street.
Mr. A Yes.
Mr. B Turn left into South Road.
Mr. A Yes.
Mr. B Turn right. You can see the cinema.
Mr. A How far is it?
Mr. B Oh, about three hundred metres.
Mr. A Thank you very much.
Mr. B Not at all.

74

Mrs. C	Excuse me. How do I get to the library, please?
Mrs. D	Go along North Road.
Mrs. C	Yes.
Mrs. D	Turn left into School Road.
Mrs. C	Yes.
Mrs. D	Turn right into River Street. You can see the library. It's on your right.
Mrs. C	How far is it?
Mrs. D	Oh, about three hundred and fifty metres.
Mrs. C	Thank you very much.
Mrs. D	Not at all.
Mrs. E	Excuse me. How do I get to the swimming pool, please?
Mrs. F	Go along East Road and turn right into High Street. You can see the swimming pool. It's on the right.
Mrs. E	Thank you. How far is it?
Mrs. F	About four hundred metres.
Mrs. E	Thank you very much.
Mrs. F	Not at all.

Say and spell:

1   or   door   short   story   water

2

a storm   a quarter

a horse   morning   pouring

75

1

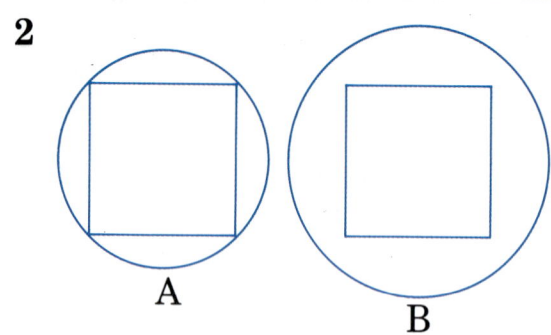

Is the small white square bigger than the small black square?

No, the black square is as big as the white square.

They are the same size.

Measure them and see.

2

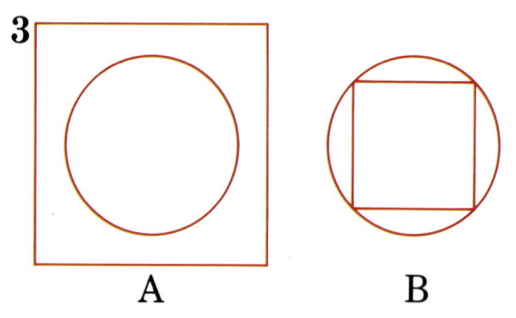

A

B

Is circle B bigger than circle A?

Yes, circle A is not as big as circle B.

Is square A bigger than square B?

No, square B is as big as square A.

They are the same size.

3

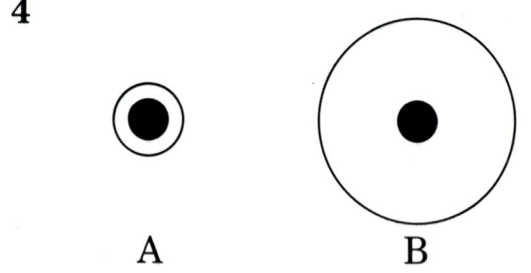

A   B

Is square A bigger than square B?

Yes, square B is not as big as square A.

Is circle A bigger than circle B?

No, circle B is as big as circle A.

They are the same size.

4

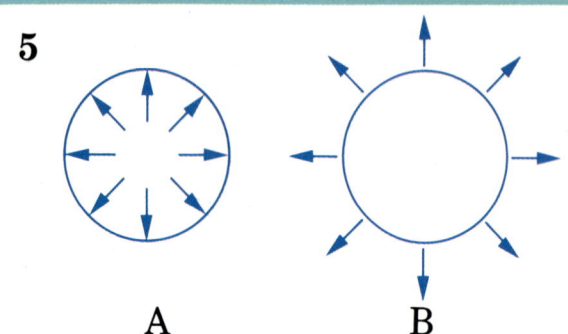

A   B

Is the black circle A bigger than the black circle B?

Measure them!

The black circle B is as big as the black circle A.

5

A   B

Is circle B bigger than circle A?

Measure them!

Circle A is as big as circle B.

Now talk about these. Then use your rulers!

1

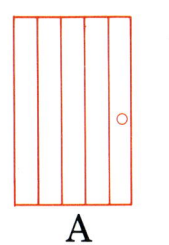 

A   B

Is door B wider than door A?

same

2

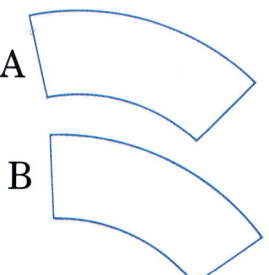

A

B

Is shape B bigger than shape A?

no

3

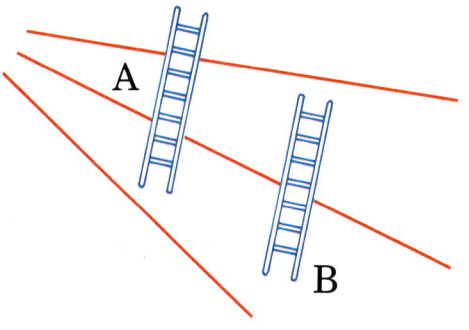

A

B

Is ladder A longer than ladder B?

no

4

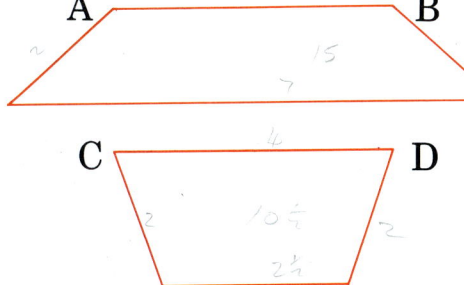

A   B

C   D

Is AB longer than CD?

yes

5

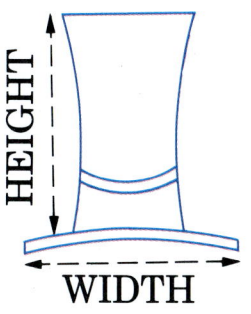

HEIGHT

WIDTH

Look at this strange hat.
Look at its *height* (how tall it is). *3cm*
Look at its *width* (how wide it is). *3cm*
Is its height greater than its width?

no

Choose the right answer.

1 Does a triangle have as many lines as a square?

A triangle has **a.** fewer / **b.** more lines than a square.

2 Does a crab have as many legs as a starfish?

A crab has **a.** fewer / **b.** more legs than a starfish.

3 Does an ant have as many legs as a spider?

An ant has **a.** fewer / **b.** more legs than a spider.

4 Does a minibus carry more passengers than a taxi?

A minibus carries **a.** fewer / **b.** more passengers than a taxi.

5 Does a car use as much petrol as a lorry?

A car uses **a.** more / **b.** less petrol than a lorry.

6 Does a television cost as much as a radio?

A television costs **a.** less / **b.** more than a radio.

7 Does a piano make as much noise as a drum?

A piano makes **a.** less / **b.** more noise than a drum.

8 Does a man weigh as much an an elephant?

A man weighs **a.** less / **b.** more than an elephant.

78

After the party

The party.

After the party.

Can you describe the room after the party? Use some of these words:

fewer	balloons cakes apples oranges bananas	less	food on the table milk in the jug lemonade in the bottles fruit on the plates noise

more	rubbish on the floor paper hats under the table empty glasses on the table

There were fewer balloons. There was less food on the table

79

The cow and the frogs

A cow was eating some grass one day. There were some frogs in the grass but the cow did not see them. It stepped on many of them but one frog was not hurt. It hopped home to tell its mother.

'Mother,' he cried. 'There was a very, very big animal in the field and it stepped on my brothers and sisters. It was very, very big.'

The mother frog blew air into the skin below her mouth. It became as big as a ball.

'Was it as big as this?' she asked.

'Oh, much bigger,' said the young frog.

The mother frog blew more air into the skin. Now it was as big as a balloon.

'Was it as big as this?' she asked.

'Oh, much bigger,' said the young frog.

The mother frog tried again. She blew and blew.

'Was it as big as this, then?' she asked.

'Oh, much bigger, mother,' said the young frog. 'Many times bigger. A hundred times bigger! You can never be as big as that animal. You will burst, like a balloon. You will never be as big as that animal.'

The mother frog became angry.

'I *will* be as big as that animal,' she said. 'I will. I will.'

She breathed deeply. Then she blew again. First

she was as big as a ball. Then she was as big as a balloon. Then she was as big as a drum! Then — BANG! She was burst! She fell down dead on the grass.

An old frog saw this.

'That is a lesson for us all,' he said. 'We must never try to look bigger or more important than we are.'

Here is the story of the cow and the frogs again, but some words have been left out. Put them in.

A cow was eating ___some___ grass. It stepped on ___some___ frogs. One ___of___ the frogs hopped home and told its mother.

'Mother,' it said. 'A very big ___frog___ stepped on us.'

The mother frog made her mouth ___as___ big as a ___ball___.

'Was it as big ___as___ this?' she asked.

'It was much ___bigger___,' said the young frog.

The mother then blew and blew. She became as ___big___ as a balloon.

'Was it ___as___ ___big___ ___as___ this?' she asked.

'It was ___much___ bigger,' said the young frog.

The mother frog tried ___again___. This time she became ___as___ big ___as___ a ___drum___. Then she burst!

We must never try to look ___bigger___ or ___more___ important than we are.

Problems and puzzles

A

Speech bubbles:
- My birthday's in September.
- I'm six months older than Betty.
- I'm two months younger than Annie. *July*
- My birthday's in May.
- My birthday's in November.
- My birthday's in the same month as Dick's. *Jan.*

January

Labels: Annie Dick Betty Emily Charles Fred

All the children are twelve years old, but some are older than others. Write down the months of their birthdays on a piece of paper. You can then answer these questions:

1 Is Betty as old as Annie?   *older*
2 Is Betty as old as Charles?   *older*
3 Is Charles as old as Annie?   *no*
4 Is Dick as old as Emily?   *older*
5 Is Emily as old as Fred?   *younger*

B One man said to another man, 'Give me a coin.
Then I'll have as much money as you.'

The second man said, 'No, you give me a coin.
Then I'll have twice as much money as you.'

$5 + 1 = 6$
$7 - 1 = 6$

$5 - 1 = 4$
$7 + 1 = 8$

1 How many coins did the first man have?   *5*
2 How many coins did the second man have?   *7*

C *How many differences are there between picture 1 and picture 2?*

D *Try to answer without measuring.*

1 Is A shorter than D?
2 Is A longer than C?
3 Is C shorter than B?
4 One line is as long as another line.
   Which one?

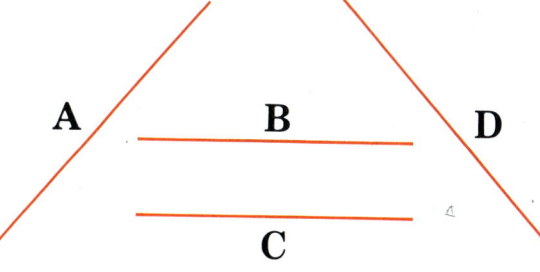

A   B   D

C

Say and spell:

Silent letters

write   wrote   wrong   whistle   listen   often

83

1

He is going to jump.

He is jumping.

He has jumped.

2

3

4

Thank you.

5

6

7

Look at page 84 and the top of this page.

What are they going to do?
What are they doing?
What have they done?

These words will help you:

1 jump into the water
2 climb the mountain
3 clean the blackboard

4 open the door
5 turn on the fan

6 switch off the television
7 paint the fence

Have you?

Answer these questions truthfully! Say: Yes, I have *or* No, I haven't.

1 Have you washed your hands today?
2 Have you washed your face today?
3 Have you combed your hair today?
4 Have you had a good meal today?
5 Have you helped your mother today?
6 Have you helped your father today?
7 Have you said 'Good morning' to your teacher?
8 Have you said 'Good afternoon' to your teacher?
9 Have you been on a bus today?
10 Have you been in a taxi today?

A game: What have we done?

1. Will you go outside, please, Sam?

2. Now, Mary, will you close the window, please?

3. I've closed it, Miss Lake.

4. Thank you, Mary. John, please move your desk.

5. I've moved it, Miss Lake.

6. Thank you, John. Sarah, will you open the cupboard door, please?

7. I've done it, Miss Lake.

8. Thank you. Mike, please turn off the fan.

9. I've turned it off, Miss Lake.

10. Thank you. Mike, please switch on the light.

11. I've switched it on, Miss Lake.

12. Thank you, Mike. Susan, will you clean the board?

13. I've done that, Miss Lake.

14. Have you really cleaned it, Susan? It is still a little dirty.

15. I've done it now, Miss Lake.

16 Come in, Sam. Now, what have we done?

17 You've switched on the light.

18 Yes, we have. What else have we done?

19 You've cleaned the board.

20 Yes, good! What else have we done?

21 You've turned off the fan.

22 Yes, we have. What else?

23 You've moved the picture.

24 No, we haven't. We haven't moved it. What else have we done?

25 I can't see anything else, Miss Lake.

26 Tell him, please.

27 Look, I've closed the window.

28 I've opened the cupboard door.

29 And I've moved my desk.

30 All right, Sam You've done well. Now, who is going outside?

Peter's busy day

Mrs. Long has gone out for the afternoon. She has asked Peter to do some work in the house. She has asked him to do these things:

wash the plates and glasses
mend the hole in the table-cloth
wash the windows
brush the floor
feed the cat
cook supper

put a table-cloth on the table
boil the kettle
open the windows
iron the clothes
switch off the television

Peter could not do all these things, but he has done his best. Look at picture 2. What has he done? What has he not done?

He has fed the cat.
He has not mended the hole in the table-cloth.

What else?

Where have they been?

the baker's shop the toy shop the bookshop the butcher's shop
the supermarket the bank

Sam has been to the butcher's shop to get some meat.
Where have the others been?

Mrs. Taylor   Sam   Mary   Mike   John   Mr. Clark

A busy family

Yesterday evening Mr. Clark came home from work at six o'clock. He was tired. He sat down in a comfortable chair. Mrs. Clark brought him a cup of tea.

'I've made some cakes,' she said. 'Would you like one?'

'Yes, please,' said Mr. Clark. 'I've worked hard today and I'm tired. What have you done today?'

'I've washed some clothes,' said Mrs. Clark. 'They're clean now. After dinner I'll iron them. I've cooked a very nice meal for you. It's fish. What else have I done today? Let me think. Oh, yes, now I remember. I've mended some socks. Your socks and John's had holes in them. You can wear them now.'

'You've worked hard today, too,' said Mr. Clark. 'Have the children worked hard? Have they helped you?'

'Yes, they have,' said Mrs. Clark. 'The girls have helped me. Mary helped me to wash the clothes and Tom helped me to cook the meal. John could not help me. His teacher gave him some homework to do. He's finished it now. Peter has mended the leg of your chair.'

'Yes,' said Mr. Clark. 'It's strong now. He's a clever boy. What has Sally done today?'

'She's cleaned all the windows,' said Mrs. Clark. 'Look, they're very clean now! We've all worked very hard.'

'Yes,' said Mr. Clark. 'You have. Now I've some good news for you. I've bought tickets for the cinema. After dinner I'm going to take you all to see a good film.'

Which picture answers the question? A, B, C or D?

		A	B	C	D
1	What time did Mr. Clark come home from work?				
2	What did Mrs. Clark bring him?				
3	What did Mrs. Clark wash?				
4	What had holes in them?				
5	What did Sally help her mother to do?				
6	What did John do?				
7	What did Tom do?				
8	Where did they go after dinner?				

Read aloud:

ed = d	**ed = t**	**ed = id**
climbed	jumped	painted
cleared	switched	mended
opened	cooked	counted
moved	washed	posted
closed	brushed	visited

91

Who is saying it?

a. That dog has bitten me!
b. That dog has knocked me off my bicycle!
c. That dog has dug a hole in the grass!
d. That dog has splashed my dress!
e. That dog has taken our ball!
f. That dog has stolen my meat!
g. That dog has spoiled my flowers!
h. That dog has made me hit a lamp-post!
i. That dog has run through the wet cement!
j. That dog has knocked me on to the ground!
k. That dog has knocked my fruit on to the ground!
l. I have had a very good day!

Mr. Clark's memory!

Which team is the best?

This is a football match.

The Blues have just scored a goal. They are a good team. They have already scored six goals. The red team has not scored any goals. The Blues are going to win the match. The Reds are going to lose.

These teams also play against the Blacks, the Yellows and the Greens. The four teams have played ten matches. Here are the results:

	Played	Won	Lost	Goals
Blues	8	8	0	18
Reds	6	0	6	3
Blacks	10	7	3	14
Yellows	9	3	6	4
Greens	8	6	2	8

The Blues have played eight matches.
They have won eight matches.
They have lost none.
They have scored eighteen goals.
They have done well.

Now talk about the other teams.

The lost ring

One evening Peter went home to his wife and said, 'You have been a very good wife. You have worked hard in the home. You have cooked me some very good meals. You have looked after the family very well. Today is your birthday and I have bought you a present!'

'Oh, thank you,' said his wife. 'This is a pleasant surprise! What have you bought me?'

'I've bought you a ring,' said Peter. He held it out for his wife to see but he dropped it.

'Oh dear!' he said, 'I've dropped it.'

He began to look for it on the floor but it was dark inside their little house and he could not see anything. He went outside and began to look for the ring in the street.

Just then a friend came along.

'What's the matter?' he asked Peter.

'I've lost a ring,' said Peter.

'I'm sorry to hear that,' said his friend. 'Let me help you to look for it. Where did you lose it?'

'Inside the house,' said Peter. 'I dropped it there.'

'Inside the house?' said his friend. 'You've lost a ring indoors and you are looking for it outdoors. I don't understand. I think that's very foolish.'

'Let me explain,' said Peter. 'It is very dark inside my house. I can't see very well. I shall never find the ring there. But out here the lamp-post gives plenty of light. I can see much more clearly. This is a much better place to look.'

Peter's friend said nothing. He looked at Peter and shook his head silently.

'Goodbye, Peter,' he said, and went away.

Here is the story of Peter and the lost ring again but some words have been left out. Put them in.

One _____ Peter said to his wife, 'You have _____ a very good wife. I have _____ you a present!'

'Thank you,' said his wife. 'What _____ you bought me?'

'I _____ bought you a _____,' said Peter. Then he _____ it.

'Oh dear!' he said, 'I've _____ it.'

It was dark _____ the house and he could not see _____. He went _____ and began to look for the ring.

A friend came along and asked, 'What's the _____, Peter?'

'I've _____ a ring,' said Peter.

'Where did you _____ it?' asked his friend.

'I _____ it inside the house,' said Peter.

'Then why are you _____ for it outside in the _____?' asked his friend.

'It is _____ inside the house,' said Peter, 'but outside there is _____ of light. This is a much _____ place to look.'

Peter's friend did not say _____ but he thought, 'Peter is very foolish.' He shook his head _____ and went away.

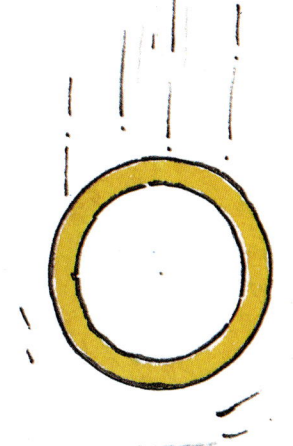

Read aloud:

I have = I've	I have not = I haven't
You have = You've	You have not = You haven't
We have = We've	We have not = We haven't
He has = He's	He has not = He hasn't
She has = She's	She has not = She hasn't
They have = They've	They have not = They haven't

Look what I've done!

What are they saying? Use these words:

drawn a map	caught a fish	fallen off my bicycle	dropped a glass
made an aeroplane	bought a new shirt	won a prize	torn my dress

Verb list

Most verbs have endings like these:

Every day I open the window.
Yesterday I open**ed** the window.
Now I have just open**ed** the window.
Every day I clean the blackboard.
Yesterday I clean**ed** the blackboard.
Now I have just clean**ed** the blackboard.

The following verbs are different. Learn them. (The ones marked with a ∗ , can also end in -**ed***.)*

Simple present	Simple past	Present perfect	Simple present	Simple past	Present perfect
Every day I …	Yesterday I …	Now I have …	Every day I …	Yesterday I …	Now I have …
am	was	been	find	found	found
begin	began	begun	fly	flew	flown
bend	bent	bent	forget	forgot	forgotten
bite	bit	bitten	get	got	got
blow	blew	blown	give	gave	given
break	broke	broken	go	went	gone
bring	brought	brought	grow	grew	grown
build	built	built	have	had	had
burn	burnt*	burnt*	hear	heard	heard
buy	bought	bought	hide	hid	hidden
catch	caught	caught	hit	hit	hit
choose	chose	chosen	hold	held	held
come	came	come	hurt	hurt	hurt
cut	cut	cut	keep	kept	kept
dig	dug	dug	kneel	knelt	knelt
do	did	done	know	knew	known
draw	drew	drawn	learn	learnt*	learnt*
drink	drank	drunk	leave	left	left
drive	drove	driven	lend	lent	lent
eat	ate	eaten	lose	lost	lost
fall	fell	fallen	make	made	made

Simple present	Simple past	Present perfect	Simple present	Simple past	Present perfect
Every day I…	Yesterday I…	Now I have…	Every day I…	Yesterday I…	Now I have…
meet	met	met	spell	spelt*	spelt*
pay	paid	paid	spend	spent	spent
put	put	put	stand	stood	stood
read	read	read	steal	stole	stolen
ring	rang	rung	stick	stuck	stuck
run	ran	run	sweep	swept	swept
say	said	said	swim	swam	swum
see	saw	seen	take	took	taken
sell	sold	sold	teach	taught	taught
show	showed	shown	tear	tore	torn
shut	shut	shut	tell	told	told
sing	sang	sung	think	thought	thought
sink	sank	sunk	throw	threw	thrown
sit	sat	sat	understand	understood	understood
sleep	slept	slept	wear	wore	worn
smell	smelt	smelt	win	won	won
speak	spoke	spoken	write	wrote	written